LIGHTNING BOLT BOOKS™

Hero Law Enforcement Dogs

Jennifer Boothroyd

Lerner Publications • Minneapolis

For Brianna

Lerner Publications Company
A division of Lerner Publishing Group, Inc.
241 First Avenue North
Minneapolis, MN 55401 USA

For reading levels and more information, look up this title at www.lernerbooks.com.

Library of Congress Cataloging-in-Publication Data

Names: Boothroyd, Jennifer, 1972- author.
Title: Hero law enforcement dogs / Jennifer Boothroyd.
Description: Minneapolis : Lerner Publications, [2017] | Series: Lightning bolt books. Hero dogs |
    Includes bibliographical references and index.
Identifiers: LCCN 2016010669 (print) | LCCN 2016017227 (ebook) | ISBN 9781512425420 (lb :
    alk. paper) | ISBN 9781512428001 (eb pdf)
Subjects: LCSH: Police dogs—Juvenile literature. | Detector dogs—Juvenile literature.
Classification: LCC HV8025 .B596 2017 (print) | LCC HV8025 (ebook) | DDC 363.28—dc23

LC record available at https://lccn.loc.gov/2016010669

Manufactured in the United States of America
1-41310-23254-4/29/2016

Table of Contents

Patrol Dogs

Did you know dogs can be police officers too? They are called K-9 officers. K-9 officers and handlers work together to keep people safe.

K-9 is short for *canine*, which means "dog."

A K-9 handler and his patrol dog are partners. The K-9 handler is responsible for taking care of his partner.

Handlers wash and feed their K-9 partners.

Always ask a K-9 handler before touching a patrol dog.

K-9 patrol officers look for suspicious activity. They work at large events and in other busy areas. You might see a K-9 officer at your school.

Handlers and their K-9s are sometimes asked to find a suspect that has run away. The patrol dog will follow commands to stop the suspect.

These officers are looking for a suspect.

Patrol dogs sniff out evidence.

K-9 patrol officers also search for evidence. Some patrol dogs bark when they find something.

Patrol dogs are very well trained. They need to obey their human partners.

Patrol dogs need to be able to go anywhere. They learn to climb.

German shepherds and Belgian Malinois are common kinds of patrol dogs. These dogs are large, strong, and smart.

Bomb-Detecting Dogs

Bomb-detecting dogs sniff out dangerous chemicals. They keep us safe!

Detection dogs use their sense of smell to find bombs.

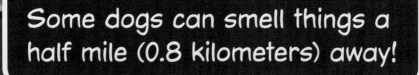

Some dogs can smell things a half mile (0.8 kilometers) away!

Dogs have an amazing sense of smell. It is much stronger than a human's.

Labradors and other retrievers are very good at smelling. They can be good detection dogs.

Detection dogs can be trained to smell many different kinds of explosives.

Detection dogs learn to search buildings, vehicles, and even people. These officers are checking shipping containers.

When the dog smells
something illegal, it sits
next to the container. Then
the dog's partner knows to
check the container.

Arson-Detecting Dogs

This building was badly damaged by a fire. The fire investigators think someone started the fire on purpose. They will call in the arson detection team.

Arson is when someone starts a fire on purpose.

Arson-detecting dogs are trained to smell chemicals that can start fires.

It can take humans days to do the work an arson-detecting dog can do in less than thirty minutes!

Arson detection teams
work carefully. Walking
through burned buildings
can be dangerous.

When the dog smells something, it lets the handler know. The K-9 is trained to not scratch at the spot. Scratching can destroy the evidence.

Arson dogs point their noses at the suspicious spot.

An investigator works to find out what chemical started a fire.

The fire investigators take samples from the spot. They will bring them to a lab. There the investigators test the samples to learn what started the fire.

Customs Dogs

K-9 officers work for the US Customs and Border Protection agency. The agency protects you from dangerous people and materials when you travel.

Customs dogs help keep travelers safer.

Many K-9 customs officers work in airports. Customs dogs have been trained to smell things that are prohibited.

Customs dogs also work at cruise ship terminals and cargo warehouses.

When a customs dog smells something, it lies down or sits next to the bag. The human customs agents will look inside the bag.

Sometimes a dog might find prohibited fruit. Customs dogs are also trained to find illegal drugs.

People often use other scented things to hide the smell of drugs. But this rarely stops the dogs from finding them.

These beagle officers have been nicknamed the Beagle Brigade.

Beagles are often used as customs dogs. They are excellent at finding scents.

Law enforcement dogs usually work for six to eight years. Most retired dogs are adopted by their handlers.

This dog is part of the family!

History of Law Enforcement Dogs

Did you know people have used dogs for protection for thousands of years?

- European police officers used dogs in the late nineteenth century. K-9s were used to control crowds. The dogs would also search for suspects.

- The New York City Police Department started using dogs in 1907. It was one of the first K-9 units in the United States.

Top Dog

K-9 officer Zeke is a Belgian Malinois. He works with Officer Tyron Meik at the Harrisburg Police Department in Harrisburg, Pennsylvania. In March 2013, Zeke and Tyron were called to help catch a suspect. During the case, the suspect shot Zeke in the neck. Zeke was flown by helicopter to a veterinary hospital. Less than two months later, Zeke was back at work with Tyron.

Officer Tyron takes Zeke home for some rest.

Glossary

detect: to notice when something is around

evidence: items or information that proves how something happened

handler: a human officer that works with law enforcement dogs

investigator: someone who searches for evidence

obey: to follow directions

prohibited: not allowed

retired: no longer working

suspect: a person believed to have broken a law

suspicious: believed to be involved in something dishonest

Further Reading

Bellisario, Gina. *Let's Meet a Police Officer*. Minneapolis: Millbrook Press, 2013.

FBI: Kids—About Our Dogs
https://www.fbi.gov/fun-games/kids/kids-dogs

Feldman, Thea. *Sadie: The Dog Who Finds the Evidence*. New York: Simon Spotlight, 2014.

Hoffman, Mary Ann. *Police Dogs*. New York: Gareth Stevens, 2011.

How Police Dogs Work
http://people.howstuffworks.com/police-dog.htm

US Fire Administration—Accelerant Detection Canines
https://www.usfa.fema.gov/prevention/outreach/canine/facts.html

Index

Photo Acknowledgments

The images in this book are used with the permission of: © otsphoto/Shutterstock.com, p. 2; © Leonard Zhukovsky/Shutterstock.com, p. 4; © iStockphoto.com/Ron Bailey, p. 5; © Mikael Karlsson/Alamy, p. 6; © Radius Images/Alamy, p. 7; © iStockphoto.com/Jan Tyler, p. 8; © Cynoclub/Dreamstime.com, p. 9; © agentry/iStock/Thinkstock, p. 10; © Jim West/Alamy, p. 11; © Tina Rencelj/Shutterstock.com, p. 12; © Isselee/Dreamstime.com, pp. 13, 31; © Getty Images North America/Getty Images, pp. 14, 15, 17; © Queen soft/Shutterstock.com, p. 16; © The Image Bank/Getty Images, p. 18; © ZUMA Press Inc/Alamy, p. 19; © wavebreakmedia/Shutterstock.com, p. 20; © michaeljung/iStock/Thinkstock, p. 21; © Scott Barbour/Staff/Getty Images, p. 22; © Monika Wisniewska/Dreamstime.com, p. 23; © 614 Collection/Alamy, p. 24; © Ilene MacDonald/Alamy, p. 25; Norm Betts/REX/Newscom, p. 26; © iStockphoto.com/FlairImages, p. 27; AP Photo/Mark Pynes/The Patriot-News, p. 29.

Front cover: © Cindy Jenkins/Shutterstock.com.

Main body text set in Billy Infant regular 28/36. Typeface provided by SparkType.